la douleur exquise

poems by

j.r. rogue

La Douleur Exquise

For every lover who has
tasted the unrequited kind,
too many times.

The Stain Soulmates Leave Behind

Entry 1

I collect my
weakness in jars
& they sure look
pretty on my shelf

the one with your
flawless little name
on the label,
will never collect dust

I always pull it down
& my thumbs wipe it clean
& my arms pull it close
& my silly sad sanity slips

& I pretend
you love me too

Entry 2

this
morning

you splayed your fingers
on the tile as
I pressed into your tired shoulders.
I watched some of the world
roll down your spine
with the shower spray.
you moaned lightly
      & I pursed my lips.

tomorrow
morning

I will practice not loving you.

Entry 3

I am living,
    no longer
        lingering in what
           I hoped we could be.
I am calm,
    no longer frantic—
       fumbling for
       the fantasy of us
that was always floating
       in the peripheries
       of my vision.
I am...
    almost-acceptance.

Entry 4

I never asked for this.
no, I never asked to
fall in love with you.

I never asked for my world
to be flipped around,
for hearts to be broken
simply because you exist.

for me to find
a new place to sleep at night,
& for most of those
nights to be restless.

for friends & family
to question my sanity.
for me to ache most days,
questioning it myself.

for you to kiss me,
putting every past lover to shame.
for your skin to be the
only softness capable of bringing
forth my own.

Entry 5

almost lovers
full mouth kisses
empty promises
    dropped silently
      into the bathroom trash

my scent scrubbed
    off your exhausted sex

I clench my eyes
& pretend I don't
hear you
retreating from
my life

call me "friend" again
&
    watch my eyes
      as all the light
        exits the room

Entry 6

you draw my heartache
on the side of your black coffee cup,
two blocks from the coast
every other Wednesday or so.

oh you love the lost, too much.

I think I can feel it
most days
in the in-between;
you spell my name in strange
ways— *b l a m e.*

I begged you for a last kiss.
I begged you &
I got it.

I begged &
I can still taste your pity.

Entry 7

I spent most of last night
on that concrete slab in
my back yard I named
"the chill spot."

no one comes over,
no one smokes out
there or passes my
bottle back to me.

I set it in the grass,
& pretend that was
my last *last* sip.

then I marry my lips to
the rim again & fall over
laughing.

I wonder if my mouth
tasted different to you.

not like a woman
of thirty who had
fallen into

convenience five or
six times & called it "love."

maybe I just tasted
like something new to write about.
a handful of fucks
& I am born again,
believing in things
I never actually believed in.

soulmates &
stained bedsheets,
your letters next to mine
on locks locked over
a Paris bridge we will
never see.

I put my mouth to
your aching neck,

I tasted salt & boredom.
I told myself it
was a second cousin
to love
& close enough.

well, maybe in our

next life.

for now I'll just be
that thirty-year-old
mistake you write
about on your off
days.

Entry 8

The pads of my feet
made love to
the street at a brisk pace—
to keep up with the strides
of the stranger who promised
to take me away from it all
for a while.

a shot of regret,
a vow to get
over you.

the rain crawled
from its concrete
grave to my knees
that no longer
prayed for your affections.

I believe the sky is crying for
us & what we will never be.

j.r. rogue

Drinking Games

my elbow is raw.
my index finger worries it,
attempting to scrape
the regret off before
it lands on that
familiar bar top.

moonshine cherry kisses.
the part of me that
misses
        you,
stored away for a later day.

I swear I'll win this game
one of these days.

What Happens In...

I twisted my ankle last night.
I broke a heel.
(new pumps.
what a bitch.)

faces blur under sin city lights.
liquor & laughter lingers
& I don't know how I
crawled back to this bed alive.

the Vegas heat beyond
the Venetian blinds calls to me,

so I count the bruises
& ignore her plea.

(I know tonight will
be rinse & repeat.)

I only wanted a goodbye.
now I'm crossing
another lover
off my list.

his initials are carved next to yours.
his letters aren't nearly as deep.

In Memoriam

who will deliver my eulogy?
I can see judgement,
stares,
mourners.

falling for you was a sin,
& small towns remember them.
you see, they have vaults filled
with transgressions.

my name,
        red ink.

& the truth is,
I care not if they forgive me.

my brief moment with you,
I shall never regret.

Fight or Flight

Departures & Arrivals

the tide is low on Tuesdays.
                    I think Poseidon knows.
the jagged rock
is always dry after I clock out
& walk the five blocks to
where we kissed for the
first time.

my feet
whisper hello & goodbye to
the water's surface
as I look for your face
in the sky.

you flew away
on a Tuesday.

I'm sure you'll fly
home then too.

Baggage Unclaimed

I pawned my heart for a
red eye flight.
I lost reciprocal &
requited.

I was too busy licking my wounds
on my layover.

now I have nothing for him &
        he knows it.

Delays & Cancellations

I flew away on a tiny jet plane.
I flew away from your
                black hole quiet.
there's un-forgiveness
climbing up your spine.
I had to go before it covered
your eyes.

it's turning cold again in the city
        & I see
        your silhouette on all the streets
        you've never visited.
this is a kind of missing I have
        never known.

did you feel it that day?
        I placed my fingertips on your
        forearm
                & everything lined up.
my soul harmonized to yours.

there's a tether connecting us.
it moves
under city streets &

mid-America fields;
from the tips of my toes
to your leaving heel.

I'm by the phone waiting
for forgiveness.
waiting for you to
be ready.
waiting.
all my life I'll be
waiting for you.

Holding Pattern

I kept waiting for him
to want me to return.
I didn't have my fill.
I didn't feel my desire dwindling.

I'd fly home just to run some
errands & tidy my room,
just to fly
back to him again.

I'd spend my last dollar.
I'd sell all my possessions.
but he never asked.

perhaps my
memory began to fade as soon
as I took my seat on the plane.

perhaps 70-some hours & change
was all he really needed of me.
perhaps I will always fly
for the heartbreak-kids.

The Devil, Denial, & Day Terrors

11:11. *make a wish.*
I bruised my wrist.

slam slam slam on the bar

another shot please?
"it's happy hour somewhere,"
the Devil whispered
in my ear as
he pushed my hair aside &
told me the widower by the sea
may love me again.

in seven or so Sundays

his lies tasted best chased
with salt & sour smiles.

in the meantime, I've been
sleepwalking from
strangers' beds.

tell me his deceit will
blossom into half-truths.

tell me I can make
my way back to you.

Shallow Depths

you create a spark—
with your touch,
with all you do,
& who you are.

your lips. your leaving.
Lichtenberg scars
& heart bleeding.

still, she reads Bukowski
to impress you.
to prove her depths.

the kind you don't swim in—
the one thing she can't grasp.

but who am I to say a thing?
when I am always
standing in the rain,
on the nights I,
too,
hear your name.

Anchor Eyes

I said it in the beginning
　　　　to whomever would listen

that I wasn't the kind of woman
who could hold the attention
of a man like that
　　　　for more than a few days

　　maybe he saw anchors in my eyes

I need to know his beauty exists
out there
& I hope no woman
ever tries to tame him

　　I'll compare the rest to him, I will

his presence is essential to me
　　　& I never lived
　　　　until I knew him

Driftwood

this bar is a harbor,
     so I'll dock my soul for the night.

you know I'm looking for you,
     most moons,
     you do not show.

don't worry, I'll take a shot for you
     & wait for you to
     drift back
         too.

The Lies We Tell

Part 1

"I want you. I miss you. I have fallen
so fucking hard for you."

I pull the pillow tight against
my tired skull,
but still I hear the soft drop of
his words awakening
my skin—flushed ruby.
I shut my eyes
& count our moments.

"you can break me open.
if anyone can. it will be you."

> "you make me feel things
> I've never experienced."

"please, don't go anywhere."

the streetlight is winking at me.
it's smirking,
beyond my broken blinds.

"why do we lie to ourselves?"
    it laughs.

Part 2

broken hearts,
& my name jotted
on the dotted line.

a new lease & a new life.
a new identity with a new possibility.
plane tickets, your mouth,
& tangled bed sheets.

I wrecked it all
for the chance to touch you,
to love you without remorse.
in return I received your silence,
& a harsh reality.

the fantasy of me,
was sold easily.
the flesh-&-bone me,
was discarded wordlessly.

I'll never fall for a lie
like that one again.
I'll never fall for words like yours.

I'll never weep for
someone who didn't care
enough to tell me why.

Part 3

tell me the-day-in
and-day-out with you
is horrid.
tell me you leave the
toilet seat up and
you forget to clean
the wax from your ears.

tell me I'll become uninterested
and really, you're quite a dull lover.

tell me you will
stop holding my hand
and your fascination
with me will fade.

tell me the soft tone of your
voice will float away,
replaced by silence and
bored bedroom eyes.

tell me anything you wish.
anything to kill my desire.

I romance you,
and you regret me.

lend a hand and help me stand
with you, on the same page.

Part 4

my favorite moments were the ones
I would allow myself to
chew on the lie.

it tasted like blood red cherries
in the summer
as it swam around my gums.

I let it stain my fingers &
the edges of my t-shirt as
I pulled it over my head
& pulled you closer.

I knew you were
merely a moment-man,
       so I closed my eyes &
           enjoyed the ones you
           gave me.

Part 5

you said you were falling;
I said the same.
it was beauty & it
was smiles & it was
nothing I had ever known.

then, suddenly, it was
friendship with a pinch
or two of flirting.

& my fear
      turns me to stone.

we both know
I'll never ask why.

Your Sadness

the beautiful man who lives
by the bay,
wants to give me a chance

a chance to be
the smiling-kind

the happy-little-
shining-kind

he wants to release
the ink from my eyes,
to drain you from my veins

he has a glossy little
two story
storybook
haven where
I can heal in

the beautiful man who lives
by the bay, no, I can't have him

I'm in love with my madness

I cannot consume his resplendence

I only want you;
your lips &
your beautiful
sadness

Swan Song

we write sad songs better
than the rest.
our niche. our place in this mess.
let me say goodbye to you?
let me stretch it out?

a day or two,
the boardwalk,
& the Atlantic.
neon orbs painting your skin
on mine
for a while.

touch me. make me sing.
don't worry that I'll hold on.
don't worry that I'll pull hope
from your parted lips.

I am resigned. I am resolute.

I won't cry this time.
not while you're
standing in my room.
not while your gaze

is turned my way.

I'll save it for a rainy day.
& you can go back to
acting as though there was
never anything between us
in the first place.

Six Degrees

the morning sun
covered you in a canary canvas.

so I drew nearer to you
& drew lines
all over your feather skin.

connect the dots.

between our past
& our meeting,

& our fall
& your leaving.

yes.
you were beneath me,
but so long gone.

Paper Cuts

Part 1

I'm in love with a coward & a thief.
a romantic with these damned
despondent eyes
I cannot break away from.

I plunged my fist through his
paper thin promises.

he blinked. he ran.

an inch of something akin
to forever was inked in my iris.

he clenched. he ran.

& I will never
forgive him.

Part 2

I have these pretty paper men
following me from tree to tree.
they want to love me.
they are pretty.
pretty on paper.

long legs for chasing
& strong arms for turning me
to face them.

I bet they would feel nice,
bare & breathless, by my side.

but they, are not you.
they can't make me sing
the way you used to.

j.r. rogue

Willow Weeping

I remember our
     last kiss,
     under that
     old willow
     tree.

you left us
     both
      weeping.

Amnesia

he took me three times last night
& once this morning.

the things he whispered...
his future plans for my flesh;
ropes,
      & knots,
          & exposure.
I reddened.
I heated.

he pressed his lips to my
core &, for a moment,
I forgot your name.

The Heavy

I can feel the heavy.
I am still wrapped in my sheets
& I feel it.

not the heavy I want;
the weight of you above me
the feel of your tender back beneath
my wanting fingertips...
no, not that.

it's the weight of you deciding
I wasn't much more than
a silly crush
& a passing fancy.

that's what I feel.
        I feel it.

Microscopic Moments

it's okay,
      it is.

it's okay
      that you do not
            love me.

I am lucky,
      I am.

I am lucky
that for a fleeting moment
you thought

      maybe you could.

Return to Sender

Letter 1

I wrote you a letter.

I wrote down everything
I could never
find the courage to tell you—
    how your silence splits me,
    how numb I am now,
    how I am letting go.

when I came home today,
I noticed
the mailman had missed
the envelope with your name
scribbled in my sloppy scrawl.

so, I dropped it in the trash.

maybe there are some things
the universe doesn't
want you to know yet.

Letter 2

I want to write a poem.
I want to write a poem about
how I feel,
how I felt,

wrapped in my fresh sheets
today,
mid-day,
blinds shut,
phone on silent.

I want to write a poem.
I want to write a poem about my
tears & the red of my face
& the black of my heart.

I want to write a poem
but I,
  am too frozen.

Letter 3

they will write stories about how
we found each other.
(the kind that piss people off.
because they don't believe it's true.
because they want it for themselves.)

& I will write stories about
        how we lost each other.
(because that's the part I will never
get over. that's the part I know best.)

& he will write stories
about the delicate
moments in
between.

(in those you will find my
love for him.)

Letter 4

I ache.
my temple
pounds.
I see stars,
but they don't glitter
the way they did last night
under the downtown lights.

my mouth,
an arid arena.

words never said to you
compete with the taste
of him
still
lingering
in my throat.

j.r. rogue

Phantom Limb

he said I had Gotham eyes,
then he bit my lip
& smacked my ass.
he didn't draw blood
& he didn't draw me out
in the way he had hoped.
not in the way you did.

you wound my dark hair
around your fist &
made me cry out.

it was with the same force
he used on me.

but behind yours was
a wildness I couldn't find anywhere
but in the depths of your eyes
& within
the way you shivered when my
lips grazed your neck.

I felt safe in
your unknown.

I was forever falling
into you, even in the arms of others.

Lipstick & Illusions

you bewitch me.
my lipstick stains
      have become prayers.
my fingertips
parade all over pleasant
men who *lovelovelove*
        my resenting flesh.

it is not you who touches me
on Sunday mornings.

I kneel beside
foreign beds
& beg them to
forfeit this ill illusion.

they do not feel as you do.
they take the magic you
left & dim me in
their dim rooms,
as I hide *lastlastlast* tears.

Code Blue

I feel November,
when I lie on the operating table.

I stretch myself out;
shoulder blades—
        lonely capsized mountains.
vertebrae—
                a sting.
my heels—
                pressed.

I cut myself down the middle.
one long incision.
the shock has me numb.
I cut out the love
that remains for you.

I place it in the gun metal
bin next to my limp wrist.
discarded.

I stitch myself up.
your favorite song plays over the
speaker in the waiting room.

I hum your lonely tune.
I wipe you from my cheeks.
your salt, your letters.

maybe it's the chill in the room.
maybe it's not you,
rolling around in my wounds.

maybe this is
the last time, too.

J.R. ROGUE is very active on social media and encourages you to follow her around.

Instagram

https://www.instagram.com/j.r.rogue/

Facebook

https://www.facebook.com/jrrogueauthor/

Facebook user group

https://www.facebook.com/groups/
1627799237440695/

Twitter

https://twitter.com/jenR501

Website

www.jrrogue.com